D1503477

DISCARD

Duxbury Free Library

Duxbury , Massachusetts

THE WAY WE WERE
NEW ENGLAND

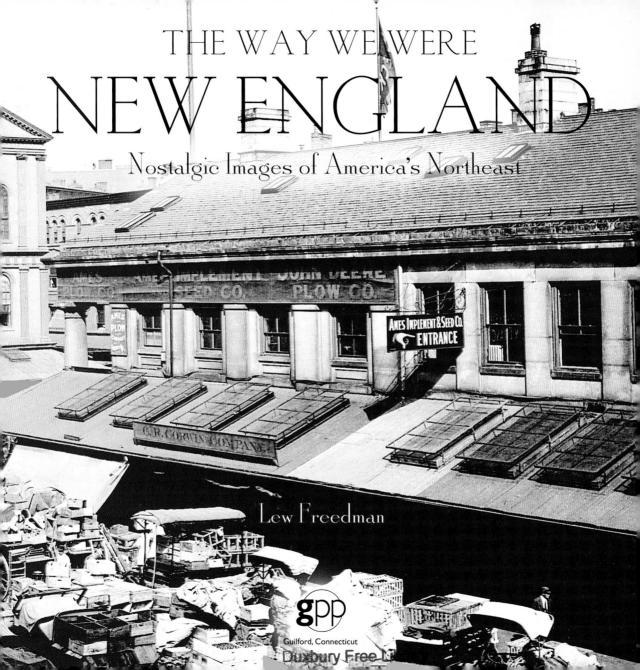

THE WAY WE WERE
NEW ENGLAND
Nostalgic Images of America's Northeast

Lew Freedman

gpp

Guilford, Connecticut

Duxbury Free L

To buy books in quantity for corporate use or incentives, call (800) 962-0973 or e-mail premiums@GlobePequot.com.

Copyright © 2010 by Compendium Publishing, Ltd

ALL RIGHTS RESERVED. No part of this book may be reproduced or transmitted in any form by any means, electronic or mechanical, including photocopying and recording, or by any information storage and retrieval system, except as may be expressly permitted in writing from the publisher. Requests for permission should be addressed to The Globe Pequot Press, Attn: Rights and Permissions Department, P.O. Box 480, Guilford, CT 06437.

Design: Compendium Design/Angela and Dave Ball
Project manager: Martin Howard
Editor: Joshua Rosenberg
Photo credits: Corbis pp 6 (Michael Freeman), 8T (PoodlesRock), 10 (Blue Lantern Studio), 20 (David Pollack/K.J. Historical), 22 (Robert Holmes), 28B (Lake County Museum), 32T (Aladin Color, Inc.), 34L (Ron Chapple Stock), 34R (James Marshall), 35T (Bob Krist), 36–37 (Bob Rowan; Progressive Image), 46B (Walter Bibikow), 50B (Swim Ink 2, LLC), 53T (Robert Holmes), 56R, 58 (G.E. Kidder Smith), 70 (Photo Collection Alexander Alland, Sr.), 71 (Catherine Karnow), 93B, 95R, 117 (Steve Lipofsky), 122B (K.J. Historical); Bettmann/Corbis 8B, 9, 10–11, 14T, 14B, 15, 17T, 17B, 18–19, 231, 35B, 45T, 47, 48R, 49T, 52, 53B, 54, 56L, 57, 80, 83, 87, 88L, 89, 90, 91, 92, 94, 95L, 96L&R, 95, 98TL, 100, 101TL, TR&B, 106T&B, 108B, 116B, 119, 120TL&TR, 121, 123, 127B; Underwood & Underwood/Corbis 32B, 48L, 50T, 72, 74, 77T, 93T, 107, 108T, 112B; Brooklyn Museum/Corbis 12B, 39B; Kevin Fleming/Corbis, 23, 113, 127T; Library of Congress Prints & Photographs Division (details available from publisher) pp 1, 4, 12T, 13, 16, 21, 24, 25T&B, 26, 26T&B, 28, 29, 30, 33, 39T, 40, 41, 42, 43TL&TR, 43B, 45B, 46T, 49B, 51, 59, 60, 61, 62T&B, 63, 64, 65, 66, 67T&B, 68–69, 73, 75, 76, 77B, 78–79, 78B, 79B, 81TL, TR&B, 82, 84–85, 86, 88R, 98TR&B, 99, 102T, BL&BR, 103, 104TL&TR, 105, 109, 110, 111T&B, 112T, 112–113, 114, 115T&B, 116T, 118T&B, 120B, 122T, 122–123, 124, 126; TopFoto 7 (Spectrum/HIP).

Library of Congress Cataloging-in-Publication Data

Freedman, Lew.
  The way we were New England : nostalgic images of America's Northeast / Lew Freedman.
      p. cm.
  Includes index.
  ISBN 978-0-7627-5453-3
  1. New England--History--20th century--Pictorial works. 2. New England--Social life and customs--20th century--Pictorial works. I. Title.

  F5.F64 2009
  974'.043--dc22

                                        2009025342

Printed in China

10 9 8 7 6 5 4 3 2 1

CONTENTS

INTRODUCTION

In summer, we inhaled our tasty Joe and Nemo hot dogs (relish only, please), washed down by a bottled tonic, and finished with a dish of Brigham's chocolate ice cream with jimmies sprinkled on top; we felt the world would never be better. On weekends, we tested the Revere Beach roller coaster's dips and turns, and felt the Atlantic Ocean's waves break on our ankles as we walked the sandy and rocky shore just north of Boston, the city of freedom in our history books that called itself the "Hub of the Universe." It was the capital of Massachusetts, for sure, and the largest city in New England by far.

Our ancestors were hardy pilgrims. They fled England to find religious freedom, stumbled into oppressive taxation and a Tea Party, and became members of the original thirteen colonies that grew into the United States. They fought the British for independence after Paul Revere rode through the streets at the midnight hour, sounding the alarm, and orators such as Sam Adams spoke in fiery words.

> *"The most serious charge that can be brought against New England is not Puritanism, but February."*
>
> Writer and naturalist Joseph Wood Krutch

ABOVE: Old Sturbridge Village in Western Massachusetts is a replica of the way rural New England communities looked in the late eighteenth and early nineteenth centuries. Here, a man in period clothing walks along a dirt footpath.

OPPOSITE: The Pilgrim Fathers landed at Plymouth Rock in 1620 and founded the colony of Massachusetts. The historic rock was later covered by a monument commemorating their arduous voyage across the ocean from England.

LEFT: A 1915 postcard commemorating the Boston Tea Party. This protest against Britain's unfair taxation without representation was one of the defining events that led to the Revolutionary War.

OPPOSITE: This church on Milk Street in Boston, built in 1729 and depicted here in the 1800s, was called the Old South Meeting House. It was the starting point for the Boston Tea Party in 1773.

LEFT: Faneuil Hall is one of Boston's most enduring landmarks, dating back to 1742. Its rooms once echoed with the oratory of patriot Sam Adams, preaching independence from England. On a November night in 1960, when this photograph was taken, the famous old building was the site of Senator John F. Kennedy's final campaign address before he won the presidency.

In an age when gadgetry was limited to the reliable radio and the newfangled television set in the corner, with maybe five channels available if we tipped the rabbit ears just so, the New England we inherited seemed an unspoiled place that was rich in history. You could touch this history at Plymouth Rock, as the first European settlers to the area did in 1620 after arriving on the *Mayflower*. Or you could walk it, along Boston's 2.5-mile-long Freedom Trail, where the Old North Church bells echoed and those heroic veterans of 1776 and the Revolutionary War were buried beneath fading inscriptions lettered on thin slabs of stone. We were weaned on the Minutemen at Lexington and at Concord, where "the shot heard round the world" was fired, and on tri-cornered hats and the bravery of our forebears.

When we were young there were no twenty-four-hour stores, Sunday blue laws still prevailed, and it never crossed our minds that we were missing out because we couldn't buy cereal in the grocery store at 3 a.m. We took Sunday afternoon drives in the Studebaker, uncomplicated road trips to munch on Ipswich fried clams on Boston's North Shore.

There, we discovered beaches other than Revere, some with purer white sand. For true solitude we could retreat to Walden Pond and become one with nature.

Many of the men who built Massachusetts and the other New England states worked the sea—and those who perished were commemorated when the Gloucester fisherman's statue was raised. Each year since 1927, as part of St. Peter's Fiesta, priests had formally blessed the fleet. The fishermen produced the special bounty identified with our area. Scallops, cod, and other fish unloaded on the docks were emblematic of the fishing industry, and represented the table fare at the multitudes of prominent seafood restaurants. Maine's lobsters were consid-

ABOVE: Wish you were here! This postcard from Boston showed off a number of Revolutionary War sites and highlights of the town's history.

RIGHT: This is the Massachusetts State House as it looked in 1922, when the building was new.

ered the best in the world. It was a shame if beef was your favorite.

Grudgingly (perhaps bribed by a New England Confectionary Company four-flavored Skybar), kids piled into the car for a foray to admire autumn leaves. Truth be told, the dazzling sight of reds and oranges would eventually seduce all of them and not just because Mom told them it should. If a state line was crossed in search of brighter colors, that made the trip exotic.

ABOVE: The birthplace of Benedict Arnold in 1851. Arnold, born in 1741, was first a military hero and then became notorious as one of the United States' most prominent traitors.

BELOW: This 1873 painting by James David Smillie shows Gay Head on Martha's Vineyard, Massachusetts.

The Basketball Hall of Fame in Springfield, Massachusetts, provided a different glimpse into New England's heritage. Dr. James Naismith invented the sport at a YMCA there in 1891. Originally, basketball was a slower-paced game, requiring shots into a peach basket— slam dunks and jump shots were not imagined until much later. The state capitol building in Hartford was a highlight of Connecticut drives, the gold dome gleaming in the sunlight. Maine offered sandy beaches and wild blueberry picking, as it still does, the fruit so sweet in flavor it didn't need sugaring. Back then Vermont was just as rustic and populated more with evergreen trees than with people. New Hampshire was dotted

ABOVE: The impressive state capitol building in Hartford, Connecticut, in 1907.

with market towns and historic sites. Rhode Island, we all knew from school lessons, was the smallest state and had a Block Island, 13 miles offshore, that we always heard about on weather reports.

In Massachusetts we never feared snowstorms, but rather prayed for blizzards "wicked good" enough to cancel school. We were well aware, though, that those places "Up North"—Maine, Vermont, and New Hampshire—were deluged with far more snow. Storms were called "nor'easters" and somehow that made them seem more brutal. The northern New England states seemed a bit mysterious, with the White Mountains—dominated by the famous

ABOVE: The theme of winter in New England is usually "Let it snow, let it snow, let it snow." In this 1954 picture, some of Boston's children brave a heavy snowfall to sing Christmas carols.

BELOW: The children's version of the Winter Olympic sport of luge is sliding down snowy hills headfirst on sleds with fast metal runners. Playing outdoors in the snow comes naturally to New Englanders, like these kids from Stamford, Connecticut.

Mount Washington, at 6,288 feet the tallest peak in the region—and people who played in the snow in ways we never considered. We usually ice skated at a Metropolitan District Commission rink, but they skated on frozen ponds without walls. In Boston we had snowball fights (it was wrong to throw at cars, but we did it anyway, until someone stopped and chased us) and built snow forts. Heavy snow in New Hampshire meant the state was open for business— multitudes gathering at resorts for downhill skiing. The ski lodges presented themselves as retreats from the city, where one could ride up ski lifts and zip down major hills, and the weary could sip hot chocolate by the fireplace.

Vermont did it differently. You could ski and be grounded simultaneously on groomed trails. This was called cross-country skiing, and it allowed those who preferred slower motion to investigate the back country at their own pace while not sinking up to their cabooses in soft snow. Or you could snowshoe, just walk along on top of the snow as the Indians did in the seventeenth century.

There was something captivating about New England in the snow, especially the areas outside the city, in the

woods that poet Robert Frost so greatly appreciated. The colonial houses sat stoically as the flakes piled into drifts, protecting everyone inside in a cocoon. The more remotely you lived, the more snow you encountered. But New England had it all: four seasons in abundance. Winter brought feet of snow. Spring was over in an eye-blink. Summer could be as humid as Alabama. And autumn gave us that fleeting rush of Crayola leaves. The saying in New England went, "If you don't like the weather, wait a minute."

We were different even in the way we talked. We New Englanders had our own tongue and we spoke with broad "A's." "Hah-vahd Ya-hd" was always exhibit number one. We could be insular, too. For decades, especially in the small towns, everyone knew their neighbors, everyone left their doors unlocked, and it took quite some time for newcomers to be embraced as locals. They say that in Maine it never happened at all, no matter how long you lived in Bangor or Bar Harbor.

LEFT: Doesn't every New England community have one of these? A landmark tea kettle that yes, blows off steam, emits its vapors in March of 1956, while the city of Boston is pummeled by a late-season blizzard.

The roots of all New Englanders ran deep. We knew that Indians shared the first Thanksgiving with the fugitives from Europe. We knew that the Indians inhabited Maine, Vermont, Rhode Island, Connecticut, New Hampshire, and Massachusetts first—long before they built the world's largest casinos in Connecticut. But the term "Native American" was not yet in vogue, and appreciation for earlier cultures tended to be limited by John Wayne movies.

Our history—that of immigrants from Western Europe—was wrapped up in throwing off Britain's yoke of tyranny. Our heroes were the men who signed the Declaration of Independence. For us, the 1600s and the first half of the 1700s were written in stories such as *The Last of the Mohicans.* Our clock seemed to start ticking with founders Roger Williams in Rhode Island, John Adams in Massachusetts, Ethan Allen in Vermont, Connecticut's Nathan Hale, and John Paul Jones, Father of the U.S. Navy (who owned a house in New Hampshire), and with the French and Indian Wars rampaging through Maine. We learned early that Boston's ancient marketplace and meeting place, Faneuil Hall, built in 1742, was the

ABOVE: Bar Harbor, Maine, in the 1880s, seen from the West End Hotel on Mount Desert. Sailboats cruise through the harbor on a summer day.

OURS...to fight for

FREEDOM FROM WANT

LEFT: The populist artist Norman Rockwell painted in Vermont and Massachusetts and spoke for small-town America in works that highlighted the pleasures of rural living. The artist also helped support the U.S. World War II effort with posters like this one, produced in 1943.

BELOW: Around and around they go. The Revere Beach amusement park, by the Atlantic Ocean just north of Boston, featured all types of activities for those seeking thrills after a day of sun and sand, including this teacup ride.

"cradle of liberty" and we never had reason to doubt its truth.

Each person possesses his or her own notion of the good old days. Each of us views the world through a different prism. Somewhere in the mind there is a pleasant fuzz that clings to a certain period of time, highlighting a mix of the best of things at the best of times that can always warm us on a chilly day. Today, New England's delights are unchanged from those days we grew up in, yet memory adds an extra charm to times gone by. No one captured this in universal terms better than painter Norman Rockwell, who began painting scenes of rural America in Abington, Vermont, in 1939 and illustrated 322 *Saturday Evening Post* covers. Fittingly, Rockwell's legacy is on display at Stockbridge, not far from Old Sturbridge Village, the Western Massachusetts reenactment settlement depicting life in New England between 1790 and 1840.

LEFT: Naturalist and writer Henry David Thoreau retreated into the woods at Walden Pond in Concord, Massachusetts, in 1845. There, he formulated the thoughts that helped make Americans aware of their disappearing wilderness.

MAJOR ATTRACTIONS

Boston Garden was a palace of sport when it opened in 1928, a cousin to New York's Madison Square Garden. Located above the North Station train terminal, it became home for decades to the Boston Celtics basketball team, the Boston Bruins hockey team, the rodeo, the circus, boxing matches, and political conventions.

During so many events, for so many years, a man who seemed born elderly greeted approaching customers with the shout, "Peanuts a dime! Three for a quarter!" as he leaned against a bare wall, resting on his crutches and one good leg. For 25 cents he passed over three small brown bags filled with peanuts in the shell, no hint of salt in sight or taste. It was a bargain almost as great as the $2 seats in the upper reaches of the "Gah-den" where the Gallery Gods perched.

For sports fans there was no better show than watching Arnold "Red" Auerbach light up a victory cigar on a Friday night or a Sunday afternoon in the closing seconds of a Celtics game when the result was

"All the hills blush. I think the autumn must be the best season to journey over even the Green Mountains. You frequently exclaim to yourself, 'What red maples!'"
Naturalist Henry David Thoreau

LEFT: Come to New Hampshire for your vacation! This alluring 1958 poster was intended to woo potential tourists to the Granite State.

OPPOSITE: The White Mountains of New Hampshire are a marvelous retreat. They offer brilliant scenery and inviting hiking trails for both residents and visitors, all attracted by such scenes as this 1900 view of the Cathedral Woods in Intervale.

assured. The Bruins always finished last, until eighteen-year-old Bobby Orr came around in the 1960s and bestowed gifts of Stanley Cups. Orr was a god on ice.

We thought the Garden would live forever, but it didn't. Now memories are being created at a newer, flashier building with better sight lines, less smoke, but also less personality. The Garden wasn't the only place to see sport though. Harvard

ABOVE: The spectacular Kancamagus Highway is 26 miles of incredible beauty in rural New Hampshire. A National Scenic Byway, the road is located within the White Mountain National Forest.

University, in Cambridge, was founded in 1630 and is the nation's oldest college. On crisp mornings, rowers from crew teams, some of them Olympian in caliber, could be seen stroking with the current just as they do today. And on sunny weekend afternoons small sailboats dotted the river, barely allowing room to throw up a mainsail. Everyone in the state rooted for the University of Connecticut basketball

teams, well before men's coach Jim Calhoun and women's coach Geno Auriemma became local heroes for their ability to challenge for NCAA titles almost annually, and scalpers charged more than the cost of a few lobster dinners for tickets to either team's games.

Boston had something to offer everyone. After reading *Make Way for Ducklings*, parents might take their children

ABOVE: The House of the Seven Gables in Salem, Massachusetts. Built in the seventeenth century, it was made famous in literature by author Nathaniel Hawthorne, who also made it his home for a time.

on swan-boat rides on the ponds of the Boston Public Gardens or introduce the youngsters to the historic locations on the Freedom Trail. A convenient underground subway connected outlying areas to downtown, where shoppers stopped at Filene's and Jordan Marsh for the latest clothing. Boston and Cambridge teemed with thousands of students and the colleges' stately old buildings were an

ABOVE: Lighthouses have long been objects of fascination, whether viewed with the naked eye, photographed in black and white, or depicted in full-color images such as this 1901 picture of The Nubble in York, Maine.

attraction in their own right, as they still are. On the third Monday in April, if it was sunny, it seemed as if all of those students, their relatives, and everyone else in the Commonwealth of Massachusetts, celebrated the Patriots' Day holiday by lining streets in west suburban communities Hopkinton, Ashland, Framingham, Natick, Wellesley, Newton, and Brookline to see the country's oldest marathon. It has been estimated that more than a million people now watch the 26.2-mile Boston Marathon, established in 1897.

The Marathon was a harbinger of spring, but when it got hotter one of the best places to be was Cape Cod. There you could enjoy the sea breezes and beaches, although the shores of Maine had cooler winds and sands. For most New Englanders the coast was within a couple hours drive, though other delights and curiosities might distract them from getting there. Who really needed the beach anyway, when you could take a dip in Lake Winnipesaukee? This lake, New Hampshire's largest expanse of inland water, also came with the bonus of a bowl of New England clam chowder (never the red Manhattan chowder), as a reward for correct pronunciation. If anyone wanted

ABOVE: Now treated as a museum and open for tours, The Breakers in Newport, Rhode Island, is a seventy-room mansion. It is seen here in 1904 when it was a residence of the Vanderbilt family. Newport is home to eleven massive mansions like this, once the domiciles of the rich and famous.

RIGHT: The Memorial Arch in Hartford, Connecticut, seen in 1905. The arch, located in Bushnell Park, was built to honor the 4,000 Hartford soldiers and sailors who served during the Civil War. It was dedicated in 1886.

to buy anything stronger than a Coca-Cola, they had to dash to a state-run package store. There were no privately owned liquor stores in New Hampshire.

Leave it to Americans to turn a dark period in history into a tourist attraction. Centuries after the grim 1692 Salem witch trials, the saltbox houses of nearby Danvers still stand. Salem, which gave us an "official" witch named Laurie Cabot, has long been trying to make up for the ill-advised burnings with the guided tours that have fascinated generations of New England folk and tourists alike. Notable among the attractions is the House of Seven Gables, constructed in 1668.

Literary heritage could also be found in Hartford, the insurance capital of the world, which was also once the home of a writer named Samuel Clemens, better known as Mark Twain. His house was declared a National Historic Landmark in 1962 and opened as a museum in 1974 after considerable renovation. And after Arlo Guthrie sang *Alice's Restaurant* in 1967, and a movie of the same name

ABOVE: Gazing northeast from the tower at Abbot Hall, an observer in 1912 could see across the city of Marblehead, Massachusetts, a quaint seaside community located 18 miles north of Boston.

ABOVE: The view from high up in the golden-domed state capitol in Hartford, Connecticut, on a snowy day in 1916.

RIGHT: The Boston Public Gardens, with its swan boats, is located in the heart of downtown Boston. For many years it has attracted families on warm days.

appeared in 1969, everyone had to make a pilgrimage to Great Barrington in Western Massachusetts, more the better if it was on Thanksgiving.

Those who preferred mountains to historic sights or the coast coaxed balky cars up the 7.6-mile Auto Road to the summit of Mount Washington, in the White Mountains of New Hampshire, so they could slap a "This Car Climbed Mt. Washington" bumper sticker on them. Mount Washington is the site of the highest recorded wind velocity—231 mph—and in winter it is nearly as abandoned as the Moon. But in summers gone by, as now, intrepid climbers scaled its sides only to be greeted by the tourists who drove there, snacking in a hut at the 6,288-foot peak, and a sign in the lodge soberly explaining how more than one hundred people have died climbing the mountain.

Vermont's Green Mountains appealed to hikers who liked an easy walk up 4,393-foot Mount Mansfield, the state's highest point. For those just admiring the scenery, the shimmering blue waters of monstrous Lake Champlain, 8,234 square miles, could be spellbinding. Wildly popular for salmon and trout fishing, more than once Lake Champlain has nearly

TOP: The New England Restaurant, with its oyster bar and fish menu, offered customers fresh-from-the-ocean seafood when they stopped by for lunch in 1920.

ABOVE: It was a bigger challenge to spell the name of New Hampshire's largest lake and famous swimming hole—Lake Winnipesaukee—than it was to spend a weekend there in summer. This postcard is from 1930.

ABOVE: New England winters have always been harsh and produce snowfalls measured in feet. While it can cause many problems, the snow also makes for stunning scenery, such as on this sunny winter day in 1940 on a snow-covered farm near Brockton, Massachusetts.

ABOVE: The Portuguese section of Provincetown on Cape Cod, Massachusetts, in 1942, photographed before the community became a wildly popular resort area for visitors escaping the summer heat of Boston and beyond.

OPPOSITE: New England sports fans have been treated to the play of the best basketball team in the world in the Boston Garden. Between 1957 and 1969 the Boston Celtics won eleven world championships. Back then the Celtics featured leaping Bill Russell (6), seen here in a 1963 contest floating in to block a shot by the superstar Oscar Robertson of the Cincinnati Royals, and John Havlicek (17).

become accepted as an official Great Lake. It also possesses a tantalizing legend. Supposedly, much like those of Loch Ness in Scotland, Lake Champlain's deep waters hide a periodically surfacing, unexplainable monster named Champ. Champ is a topic of conversation, but search parties are rare.

Confident hikers from all over also make their way to 200,000-acre Baxter State Park in Northern Maine. Some are coming and some are going on the 2,150-mile footpath of the Appalachian Trail that connects Maine and Georgia. Atop Mount Katahdin, the optimistic and sore-footed alike pause, either celebrating the culmination of a magical quest or the beginning of an exhilarating journey.

New England has always been mightily influenced by the sea, and Mystic Seaport on the Connecticut coast was the place to explore that aspect of the region's history. New England whalers and shipbuilders of all sorts are commemorated in the museum there that was founded in 1929. The town also built a replica of the slave ship *Amistad*, which was made famous in a movie of the same name. When not touring or being used as a teaching vessel, the ship docks in Connecticut.

TOP: When it was hot and humid, seasonal getaways to the beach to enjoy the sand and surf were very popular. Favorite destinations included Martha's Vineyard, Cape Cod, and the Maine coast.

ABOVE: There were several ways to reach the top of New Hampshire's 6,288-foot Mount Washington, New England's tallest—on foot, by car, or by this cog railroad.

ABOVE: Vermont is tremendously proud of Lake Champlain. The huge lake, shown with the Hotel Ampersand in the background, has shaped the history, economy, transportation, and recreation of the region since long before its discovery by Europeans in 1609.

If there is one thing that New Englanders appreciate it's a good deal, and the man who stole their hearts with his sturdy, reliable line of all-weather boots was named L. L. Bean. Leon Leonwood Bean set up shop in Greenwood, Maine, in 1912 and never imagined that his store would one day become a seven-day-a-week, twenty-four-hour-a-day tourist magnet in Freeport.

Tiny Rhode Island, 37 miles wide and 48 miles long, or just 1,545 square miles in size, is conducive to day trips. It was first sighted by explorer Giovanni da Verrazano in 1524 and later became known for Newport, a moneyed community that served as a getaway for the nation's richest families. Upper-crust American clans,

ABOVE: Rhode Island is the smallest state in the Union and calls itself the Ocean State. A sailing hotbed, Little Rhody relishes its proximity to the sea.

ABOVE: Mystic Seaport in Connecticut is a maritime museum and sometimes active shipyard where the famous *Amistad* docks. These wooden lobster traps commemorate the commercial fishing industry so important to New England.

ABOVE: Newport, Rhode Island, is home to the International Tennis Hall of Fame and hosted the America's Cup sailing competitions for decades. It thrives on being perched next to Newport Harbor, and on a sunny day like this one, the water is a nearly surreal, hypnotizing shade of blue. The 11,248-foot Claiborne Pell Newport Bridge spans the harbor and Narragansett Bay.

RIGHT: John F. Kennedy loved to escape to his Cape Cod summer home with his wife Jacqueline and their children, even after he was in the White House.

"I will back up Hartford in everything else if he (the mayor) will be
responsible for the weather. It is
more beautiful than any other city
excepting Worcester (Massachusetts)
and it is the honestest city in
the world."

Mark Twain in an 1882 speech about his
home of Hartford, Connecticut

notably the Vanderbilts and the Astors,
once resided in the eleven "properties"
spread over 250 acres of gardens. As summer homes they far eclipsed overnight summer camp tents. The humongous houses,
many dating to the nineteenth century,
now operate as museums and tourist attractions and are every inch the palaces of
European royalty. The imagination can
only run riot wondering what it would be
like to reside in such a glorious manor.

LEFT: Though small, Rhode Island is home to numer-
ous universities and colleges. This is an
aerial view of the U.S. Naval War College,
on Coasters Harbor Island in Narragansett Bay.

TRANSPORTATION

For a romantic view of Portland—Maine's principal city—young people and visitors have long treated themselves to a ride on the Maine Narrow Gauge Railroad and a stop at the adjacent museum that honors the state's industrial past. Locomotives dating to 1913 are on display, reminding observers just what workhorses they were. In old Connecticut, as now, early-morning trains were filled with well-dressed commuters in their neatly pressed suits. The businessmen of Bridgeport and Stamford, New Haven and Greenwich, Fairfield and Milford, lined up ten-deep to climb aboard the trains that carried them into Manhattan each weekday to ply their trades in high finance and high-priced legal work. The names of the railroads changed with the passage of time, but the ritual did not.

This has been the way of Western Connecticut for decades. Men who choose to raise families in plush suburbs still tote their briefcases aboard the New Haven Line, or Penn Central, or Amtrak,

"Two roads diverged in a wood and I— I took the one less traveled by, And that has made all the difference."

From "The Road Not Taken," Robert Frost

skimming over sheaves of paper in the morning and imbibing post-work cocktails with ties loosened on the journey home after 5 p.m., white-collar workers in an upscale state that has always marked the dividing line between Boston and New York. Similar trains run north, as well, alongside Interstate 95, skirting New London and on into Providence, Rhode Island, before coming to rest in South Station in downtown Boston. For many, the train has always constituted sensible travel, especially for those riding into Boston, long described as a jungle for motorists.

Unlike many other major U.S. cities, which were laid out in grids and whose streets are readily deciphered because they are numbered sequentially, the center of Boston is a jumble. The city was built with horse-carts in mind. The streets cut away at angles and adopt new names at corners where least expected, and there are simply far too many vehicles squashed into the heart of the city.

ABOVE: Lighthouses, such as this one at Buzzard's Bay in Mattapoisett, Massachusetts, were built to warn of hazards to shipping, but they also became popular landmarks and attracted visitors who found them romantic reminders of New England's maritime history. Many have interesting stories and some are even reputed to be haunted.

RIGHT: Artist Albert Fitch Bellows depicted a popular pastime of the nineteenth century when he painted carriage riding through the New England countryside in 1876.

The Boston driver is a distinct species, long identified for failing to step on the brakes unless the action is absolutely imperative. Turning left after the light has turned red is a given. Aggressiveness at all times, whether darting between slower vehicles, challenging for parking spaces, or taking command on the Massachusetts Turnpike at high speed, is understood to be standard behavior. Stopping for pedestrians to cross the street is frowned upon, if only because the car behind you might not be prepared to halt without crashing into your trunk.

Those who sought to ignore the havoc of traffic might ride the MTA; the Metropolitan Transit Authority's trains were cars powered from overhead wires as they rocked along above and below ground. Later, the same operation's name was changed to the Massachusetts Bay Transportation Authority (MBTA). Today, many call it the "T" for short.

In New England, the farther one retreats from Boston the safer a driver expects to be. He or she will be expected to drive slower and will find it easier to claim a parking place. Patience is in inverse proportion to the distance. However, one's eyes must be peeled at all times in rural Maine,

LEFT: The bright light of the Portland Head Light at Cape Elizabeth, Maine, sweeps the ocean to help a passing ship avoid foundering on the rocky approach.

ABOVE: Square in form rather than round, the Watch Hill Lighthouse in Rhode Island was built in 1855 and has a granite tower lined with brick. It was first lighted on February 1, 1856.

LEFT: One of Connecticut's most attractive lighthouses is the New London, seen here in 1900.

OPPOSITE, TOP LEFT: Pecks Ledge Light in Connecticut, seen here with people on its balcony in 1906, was a little bit different from most other lighthouses because it was built offshore rather than on land.

OPPOSITE, TOP RIGHT: The Lynde Point lighthouse in Old Saybrook, Connecticut, is a statuesque, sturdy example of lighthouse construction.

OPPOSITE, BOTTOM: Seen here in 1912, Gloucester, Massachusetts, has one of the most picturesque beaches in the North Shore area and has been popular with swimmers and sailors for decades. In the background is Annisquam Lighthouse, built in 1897.

notably at dawn and dusk, to avoid unwelcome collisions with 1,000-pound moose.

Memorably green, the Mystic River Bridge (the Maurice J. Tobin Memorial Bridge) connects Charlestown, Boston, to the near North Shore and places such as Chelsea, Revere, Somerville, and Malden. Boston Harbor is a venerable port and Charlestown is home to one of the most famous ships in the world. Known as "Old Ironsides," the *Constitution* is the oldest ship in the U.S. Navy. The wooden-hulled, three-masted frigate first set sail in 1797 to combat pirates and was active in battles for decades. The public became inordinately fond of the ship, and there was a huge outcry each time the navy threatened to decommission her.

Eventually, the *Constitution* was docked in Boston and did not budge for years. For generations, schoolchildren in the area took class trips to see the restored ship, though she never left harbor. However, fully refitted and regenerated, the *Constitution* has periodically been taken out of mothballs and paraded around the world for those enthralled by tall ships. In 1997, in celebration of its 200th birthday, the *Constitution* sailed once again.

Although Interstate 93 creases New Hampshire, the network of state highways carrying visitors into the scenic countryside, is highly developed. A naturally chiseled rock formation called "The Old Man of the Mountain"—an apparent face of an elderly man—was from 1805 a cherished stopping point, before the famed five granite cliff ledges on Cannon Mountain in the White Mountains collapsed from their own weight in 2003. To date New Hampshire officials have not had the heart to take down directional signs leading to the spot.

With all of the beauty in the far-flung United States, it takes a special locale to be designated a National Scenic Byway by the U.S. Department of Transportation. One such road is the 26.5-mile Kancamagus Highway in the White Mountain National Forest in New Hampshire. Some believe is the prettiest stretch of pavement in New England.

The kids of New England thought nothing of jumping on their bicycles with hand brakes (or, if they were really lucky, on Schwinn three-speeds) and riding for hours. Most of us didn't even have kick-stands, so we just lay the bikes on the ground when we ran into the drugstore to buy a tonic, or left them on the dirt for hours while we played

OPPOSITE, TOP: Tremont Street has long been a center of commerce in downtown Boston. This is a view of the avenue in the 1870s.

OPPOSITE, BOTTOM: A look at bustling Westminster Street in Providence, the capital of Rhode Island. In 1901 with traffic consisted of electric streetcars and horse-drawn vehicles.

ABOVE: In 1904, the Clinton-Wachusett sewage and water supply system was under construction to serve the growing population of the Boston area.

LEFT: Known locally as the *On Time*, this ferry serves as an important link between Edgartown, Massachusetts, on Martha's Vineyard, and Chappaquiddick Island.

baseball at the park. Bicycle riding is still massively popular in Vermont, where the dairy farms stretch for mile after mile on back roads. Many ride from inn to inn, where each night a hearty dinner and a soft bed await. Cycling is also the best way to enjoy the fall colors. Those in-your-face leaves ripen as you pedal beneath them,

ABOVE: Construction of the subway system in progress at South Station, at the corner of Summer Street and Atlantic Avenue in Boston, in 1914. Note the old-fashioned horse-drawn carts; still in use in this simpler age.

marveling at the shades of red, yellow, and orange so vivid as they twirl through the air and come to rest on the asphalt. The bicycle rides of late summer and autumn contrast with Vermont's hard winter pastimes of cross-country skiing and snowshoeing, but year-round the beauty of the Green Mountain State beckons.

ABOVE: In the early days of flight, test pilots, solo aviators, and especially female pilots such as Australian Jessie Miller, were big news. Miller is seen here in a Stinson Detroiter at Old Orchard Beach, Maine, in the 1920s.

ABOVE: A unique form of home schooling in Crawford Notch, New Hampshire, in 1917. The railroad delivered teacher Lena Parker twice a week to the small community where the six children of Mr. and Mrs. James M. Monahan sought an education.

LEFT: Growing up in New England meant that you were going to have more than a passing familiarity with snow. It also meant it was good to learn at a young age how to enjoy winter, sometimes by taking rides in a horse-drawn sled like this one, photographed in 1921.

ABOVE: Since the early days of the railroads, New Englanders have commuted to city jobs on trains. In the age of steam, the trains were pulled by powerful locomotives like this one, built in 1900. Today, train travel remains a popular way to cover the relatively short distances within and between New England states.

RIGHT: Unless the snow became overwhelming, the trains continued to plow through all over New England, even in bitter weather. This Massachusetts train was just one of those making tracks during the winter of 1940–41.

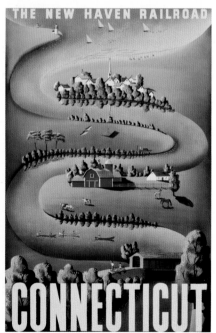

THE NEW HAVEN RAILROAD

CONNECTICUT

ABOVE: Once in a while, railroad workers dissatisfied with their working conditions went on strike, leaving commuters like these in Boston to walk to work.

LEFT: For decades, men in suits and ties rode the New Haven Railroad from Connecticut to New York City to work. Artist Ben Nason's 1941 poster highlighted some of the idyllic countryside the train passed through.

Bicycling is also a good way to catch the spectacular ocean views of Rhode Island. The state's small size is an advantage when it comes to zipping around, and visitors certainly won't need a car.

Although Clint Eastwood and Meryl Streep convinced the world that the only covered bridges left in the United States were in Iowa, there are eight in Maine; the oldest, called Hemlock and located in Fryeburg, dates to 1857. The bridges are wistful symbols of a more innocent time, as is the 1855 Baker Island Light on Mount Desert Island. It still provides navigational aid and lights memories for those who parked along the shore admiring the whitecaps rolling in. Many other Maine lighthouses are still in working order.

RIGHT: Launched in 1797, the U.S.S. *Constitution* is docked in Charlestown, Massachusetts. Usually, her job is to host tourists and elementary school children on class trips, but once in a great while, such as on this occasion in 1932, she will set sail.

LEFT: The U.S.S. *Constitution*'s glorious history is told in detail at the museum right next to the ship.

BOTTOM LEFT: New England is famous for its shipbuilding and its powerful weather. At the end of August 1954, the two collided. Winds from Hurricane Carol reached 100 mph and toppled the U.S.S. *Nehenta Bay* from its moorings in Boston.

PAGES 54–55: Many of Boston's streets were originally constructed for horse-drawn traffic and their confusing layout is a notorious cause of frustration for drivers. The building of the John F. Fitzgerald Expressway in 1955 was one attempt to modernize the city's roads.

ABOVE: With drivers who paid only loose attention to rules, Boston was never an easy place to drive around. Things only got worse when a blizzard like this one in 1956 made the roads more treacherous.

RIGHT: Once upon a time, neighborhood stores like this Thompsonville, Connecticut, shop provided all-purpose service. Here you could get everything fixed, from your bicycle or motorcycle to your car.

ABOVE: If visitors want to reach Boston (or for that matter, much of New England) by air, the place to land is Logan International Airport, shown here with its new, nearly completed, 140-foot-high control tower in 1955.

BUSINESS AND INSTITUTIONS

"Friendly's" was the perfect name. The eatery served the fried clams New Englanders devoured like popcorn, and offered so many different types of ice cream the choice stumped us. But best of all, for dessert, the Wilbraham, Massachusetts, chain offered the Fribble. America knew all about milk shakes, but Fribbles were so thick you were better off drinking them with a spoon than through a straw. They were indisputably denser than milk shakes and creamier than the frappés you could get in Boston. A chocolate Fribble was the dreamiest ice cream concoction a kid could imagine, and Friendly's remains a New England institution today.

Conservative New Englanders thought that risqué Bostonians engaged in excess and that the Hub was Sin City. At least part of it was. In Scollay Square, the drinking, carousing, and womanizing was legendary. Sailors with cash in their pockets and time on their hands knew where to go for adult entertainment. The burlesque shows of

"Your fences need to be horse-high, pig-tight and bull-strong."
The Old Farmer's Almanac

Ann Corio at the Old Howard and Sally Keith at the Crawford House packed them in, and Ms. Keith performed tricks with tassels attached to her chest. Fisticuffs with big-timers from John L. Sullivan to Rocky Marciano were staples of the area for decades, too. Once a housing district for the wealthy, in the 1900s Scollay Square became a renowned theater district featuring stage stars like Fanny Brice, George Burns, Fred Allen, and the Marx Brothers. After vice squads grew testy about the live

OPPOSITE: The Henry Whitfield House of Guilford, Connecticut, was built in 1639 and is the oldest house in Connecticut.

RIGHT: The Newport Tower, seen here in 1937, was for decades believed to have been constructed in about 1670. Now, however, some think it was built much earlier—by Vikings who may have landed on American soil long before Columbus's fabled adventure of 1492.

LEFT: A 1941 view of Old Ship Church in Hingham, Massachusetts, a Gothic-style building constructed in 1681. It is the oldest church in the state and the oldest church in North America in continuous use as a place of worship.

OPPOSITE: Slater Mill, founded by Samuel Slater in 1793 in Rhode Island's Blackstone River Valley, was a cotton mill that helped make the state a textile manufacturing center for 150 years. The valley is considered to be the Birthplace of the American Industrial Revolution.

Free Library

Duxbury Free Library

female shows, motion picture theaters and restaurants predominated. Eventually, old Scollay Square disappeared, plowed under for the Government Center area housing City Hall, among other edifices. One surviving institution is Durgin Park, where diners have eaten fried cod, Yankee pot roast, Boston baked beans, and Indian pudding since 1827.

Entertainment on the edge was shoved uptown to Washington Street, near the upscale Boston theater district that previewed plays before they premiered on Broadway. The new Combat Zone was a haven for strip-tease clubs like the Teddy Bare Lounge. The women performing in these venues would have considered Sally Keith overdressed.

Much of the twentieth century was dominated by elected officials of Irish heritage, though in the 1960s Edward Brooke became the first African-American elected to the U.S. Senate since Reconstruction. James Michael Curley, a notorious Boston mayor and governor, was immortalized as Frank Skeffington in the book and movie *The Last Hurrah.* John F. Kennedy, elected president of the United States in 1960, was the greatest achiever of the political dynasty bearing his name.

ABOVE: This huge manufacturing facility in Bridgeport, Connecticut, belonged to the Eaton, Cole & Burnham Company. It produced brass, steam, and water goods, iron filings, and tools in the midnineteenth century, all in one building.

BELOW: A color lithograph of a bird's-eye view of Willimantic, Connecticut, in 1882, with depictions of the town's most important commercial, religious, and residential buildings.

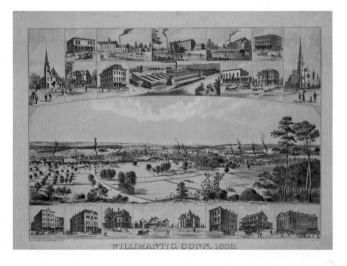

ABOVE: The stately New London Public Library in New London, Connecticut, in 1891.

Fittingly, for a major health center with the Massachusetts General Hospital at its heart, "New England's favorite charity" is in Boston. The Jimmy Fund was established in 1948 by the Variety Club of New England to fight cancer at the Dana-Farber Cancer Institute. The club arranged for a twelve-year-old cancer-afflicted boy, using the pseudonym Jimmy, to speak from his hospital bed about his baseball heroes and his illness on Ralph Edwards' nationally broadcast radio show. The Boston Red Sox have been affiliated with the Jimmy Fund since 1953.

Another notable Massachusetts organization, the Woods Hole Oceanographic Institution, is the world's largest ocean-oriented research facility. It was created in 1930 on Cape Cod.

New England also has its share of centuries-old structures. The oldest church in Massachusetts, Old Ship Church in Hingham, was built in 1681. Of English-style Gothic architecture, it is the oldest continuously worshipped-in church in North America, and currently used for Unitarian Universalist services.

The Henry Whitfield House of Guilford, Connecticut, built in 1639, is the oldest house in Connecticut. Another fascinating site is Rhode Island's Newport Tower in Touro Park. The stone structure was long believed to be a remnant of a windmill built about 1670, but scientists added spice to the debate, suggesting Vikings may have constructed it long before Christopher Columbus hit North American shores in 1492. In Derry, New Hampshire, for decades it has been possible to stop by poet Robert Frost's old farm in the woods on a snowy evening.

Also a New Hampshire company, the *Manchester Union Leader* crossed lines from business to political institution, led by arch-conservative publisher William Loeb, who attempted to set policy for the entire state. Loeb made politicians cry, and his

continued on page 71

ABOVE: The Boston area, including Cambridge, across the Charles River, is a focal point for higher education. Colleges such as the Massachusetts Institute of Technology, seen here in the late nineteenth century, attract thousands of students.

RIGHT: Phelps Hall and its signature gateway arch on the campus of Yale University in New Haven, Connecticut, in 1901.

OSBORN HALL, YALE COLLEGE.

FAR LEFT: Osborn Hall, one of the many distinctive and memorable buildings on the campus of Yale University, photographed in 1901.

TOP LEFT: The Scoville Memorial Library in Salisbury, Connecticut, seen in 1895.

BOTTOM LEFT: This magnificent structure could easily be mistaken for a state legislative building or a governor's mansion. It is the Deborah Cook Sayles Public Library in Pawtucket, Rhode Island, as seen in 1901.

LEFT: This impressive structure is the Public Library in Pittsfield, Maine, in about 1904. It was built in 1903 with a $15,000 grant from the Andrew Carnegie Foundation, $10,000 raised from the local citizens, and $5,000 donated by the estate of the late Robert Dodson.

FAR LEFT: Boston's Quincy Market in 1900.

LEFT: A market on wheels. This truck is laden with vegetables from a farm on Nantucket Island, Massachusetts.

editorial influence was the standard-bearer for the state's first-in-the-nation presidential primary.

Another of New England's best-known institutions is *The Old Farmer's Almanac*, published in Dublin, New Hampshire. The annual publication, which started in 1792 (and sold at nine cents a copy), is often relied on to predict the weather. Published continuously since 1818, it is chock full of homespun advice on gardening, cooking, fishing, and other "essentials" of life. The company maintains a secret weather forecasting formula, supposedly stored in a black tin box, and claims an 80 percent accuracy rate. People must believe it, because sales still top four million annually.

Rhode Island basks in its learned and historic status. Not only is it home to the famed Rhode Island School of Design, Ivy League Brown University, and the University of Rhode Island, but it is the Birthplace of the American Industrial Revolution. Pawtucket, in the Blackstone River Valley, is where Slater's Mill, the cotton mill built by Samuel Slater in 1793, was erected, making Rhode Island a leading textile manufacturer for 150 years. Rhode Island also claims clams of the most delectable nature, called quahogs.

With 63.6 percent of its residents describing themselves as Roman Catholics, Rhode Island has the largest percentage of Catholics of any state. The capital city of Providence is home to Providence College,

ABOVE: New England farmers have long sold their produce along the road at stands such as this one in Greenwich, Connecticut.

RIGHT: The old Massachusetts State House in Boston with its golden dome, about 1905. A new state house was opened in the capital city in 1922.

AETNA INS.   TRAVELERS INS.
WADSWORTH ATHENAEUM   MUNICIPAL BLDG.

which is administered by the Dominican Order of Friars and has a distinguished basketball tradition.

Hartford, Connecticut, was founded in 1637 and is one of the oldest cities in the United States. Its Wadsworth Atheneum is the oldest public art museum in the country, and Bushnell Park is the oldest public park. Hartford and East Hartford are separated by the Connecticut River (New England's longest at 407 miles), and the 1,192-foot-long, nine-span Bulkeley Bridge is the longest and widest stone arch bridge in the world. Opened in 1908 after an 1895

ABOVE: Men and their automobiles outside a garage in Greenwich, Connecticut, in 1908, the year that Henry Ford launched his famous Model T. He joked that the public could buy Model Ts in any color they wanted as long as it was black.

OPPOSITE: This view of downtown Hartford, Connecticut, in the early 1900s shows the Travelers insurance company's head-quarters and the Wadsworth Atheneum art museum.

fire, the bridge replaced the original 1818 covered wooden structure. Hartford, the Insurance Capital of the World, is also home to the headquarters of health insurance company Aetna. This building is not just another gleaming skyscraper—its architects drew their inspiration from Connecticut's old state house in designing what the company calls the world's largest brick colonial building. It is topped with a Georgian tower.

The University of Maine in Orono is the state university. Otherwise-taciturn Mainers will always let loose with cheers *continued on page 83*

LEFT: A team picture of sorts taken of the workers at the Seacoast Canning Company's Factory #4 in Eastport, Maine, in 1911. Much of Maine earned its living from the sea, either in commercial fishing or processing the catch. New England fishermen worked at a perilous profession to help feed the world and shipped their catch to market as fast as possible.

RIGHT: New England was a center of textile manufacturing for well over a century. These women in a South Manchester, Connecticut, workplace in 1914 are sorting and cleaning fibers from silkworm cocoons.

BELOW: Want a shoeshine, Mister? This young boy made a living as a bootblack on the streets of New Haven, Connecticut, in 1909.

ABOVE: A 1915 view of the Civic Center in Providence, Rhode Island's principal city. The current version of the downtown civic center is called the Dunkin' Donuts Center— the title sponsor is the most popular doughnut maker in New England founded in 1950 and based in Providence.

RIGHT: Tobacco was a cash crop at Huttings Tobacco Farm in Rockwell, Connecticut, in 1917. At that time, children labored in the fields for $1.50 a day instead of spending their time in school.

LEFT: In the 1920s, when there were often protests about inhuman working conditions in factories, the Cheney Silk Mills in South Manchester, Connecticut, had a reputation for favorable workplace safety.

OPPOSITE: The ornate, lovingly constructed Hotel Elton in Waterbury, Connecticut, was popular with its high-end clientele in the 1920s.

ABOVE LEFT: Cousins aged eight and ten delivering the news to pedestrians in Hartford, Connecticut, in 1924.

ABOVE RIGHT: The United Workers Boys Club, in New Haven, was a place where newsboys could congregate and play pool when not selling newspapers.

BELOW: In 1939, even the building of this Berlin, Connecticut, ice cream store looked scrumptious. There was no mistaking what was served there.

LEFT: Lawrence, Massachusetts, was for many years a manufacturing center. It is located about 25 miles north of Boston on the Merrimack River, near the New Hampshire state line. In the 1940s, rail cars constantly came and went from its factories.

RIGHT: Women working on an assembly line at the Winchester Repeating Arms Company's plant in New Haven, Connecticut, in 1946.

PAGES 84–85: Working the soil in Southington, Connecticut, in 1942 on ground owned by James Pompey. An Italian immigrant who twenty years earlier came to the United States to establish a new life, Pompey had a United Nations–type farm, worked by people from Finland, Germany, and many other countries.

for its Black Bear sports teams. Colby, Bowdoin, and Bates as institutions of higher learning are small, remote and expensive, but are still regarded as part of an elite set of colleges, the Little Ivies. Their students may dodge bears and moose before stepping into their classrooms, but that's part of the charm of northern New England.

At one time, half of America thought all men from Maine wore plaid flannel shirts. The image of Maine logging was deeply ingrained in the national psyche. English explorers first felled trees in Maine in the early 1600s, and for thousands of Maine families in the 1900s logging was still a way of life. That

lifestyle is honored at the Lumberman's Museum in Patten, and dozens of logging companies still operate in the state. It is no rarity to see a heavily laden truck roaring down the highway transporting lashed-down logs on their way to becoming someone's furniture.

Massachusetts may have exported its Friendly's, but a couple of friends—Ben Cohen and Jerry Greenfield—did that company one better when they moved to Vermont in the 1970s. Together they set up Ben & Jerry's to produce ice cream and frozen yogurt, and in doing so started a company that the state can be proud of. The only foodstuff that Ben & Jerry's can't match is Vermont maple syrup. Vermonters cannot be blamed for believing that they actually invented the sticky, sweet substance that is so intensely identified with the state.

> *"The various courses should be so arranged that, insofar as practicable, every student might study what he chose, all that he chose, and nothing but what he chose."*
>
> Brown University president
> Francis Wayland in 1850

OPPOSITE: A quiet day in Southington, Connecticut, in 1942. Atlantic Oil is selling gas on one corner and the office of the *Southington News* can be seen in the background.

ABOVE: Crossing the old stone street in Scollay Square, Boston, in 1943 during the sedate daytime. Live shows featuring everything from boxing and comedians to exotic dancers were part of the square's notorious nightlife.

ABOVE: Fanne Fox, The Argentine Firecracker, was a stripper at the Pilgrim Theater in Boston's Combat Zone where she famously met a married U.S. congressman, Wilbur Mills of Arkansas. Mills, a powerful committee chairman, had his career ruined when police stopped his car late one night in Washington, D.C., in 1974. Fox, who had been with him in the car, fled the scene and jumped into the Tidal Basin (part of the Potomac River), from which she was rescued by a policeman.

RIGHT: Bold and creative architecture was a feature of the First New Haven National Bank, which was built in Connecticut in 1958.

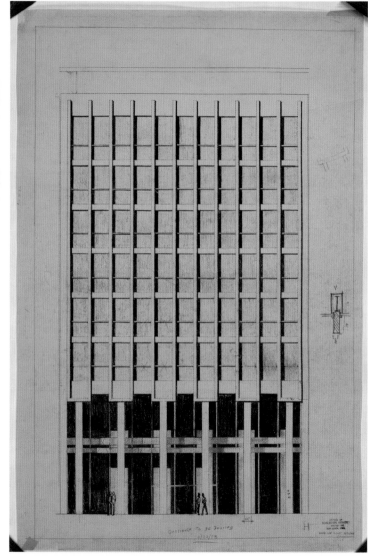

ABOVE: Decades ago, long before they were commonplace, tattoos were seen as the province of sailors and the disreputable. In Boston, tattoo parlors were a feature of the risqué entertainment district around Scollay Square into the 1960s.

ABOVE: A tree-stuffing contest on the campus of the University of Maine in 1961. A sorority and a fraternity competed to put the most humans in the tree. Thirteen women crammed in, but the men won with fifteen.

RIGHT: A 1973 aerial view of the Woods Hole Oceanographic Institution in Woods Hole, on Cape Cod, Massachusetts. The institution remains a world-famous center for research, writing, and exploration.

LIFESTYLE AND CELEBRITIES

Pride. Self-sufficiency. A sense of history. All of those are traits of men and women from New England. The region's history dates back far enough for its residents to feel that their ancestors mattered in the making of the United States. They are aware of which families came across the sea on the *Mayflower*. They point with pride to the daring of the men involved in declaring independence, who put their John Hancocks on what would be viewed by some as a treasonous document and by others as the deed to a nation.

When schoolchildren in Maine, New Hampshire, Vermont, Massachusetts, Rhode Island, and Connecticut study American history, they are studying their own neighborhood's history. Some of the most famous Americans in the country's past are the renowned intellectuals and leaders of eighteenth-century New England. They were revolutionaries and patriots in ideas, thought, and action: generals on the battlefield or statesmen writing a new constitution. John Adams

> *"New England has a harsh climate, a barren soil, a rough and stormy coast, and yet we love it, even with a love passing that of dwellers in more favored regions."*
>
> Former U.S. senator Henry Cabot Lodge

LEFT: Benjamin Franklin was one of the founding fathers of the United States. He was born in Boston, though he gained much of his fame while living in Philadelphia. This photograph of a bust of Franklin dates to 1929.

ABOVE: The birthplace of statesman Daniel Webster in Salisbury, New Hampshire. Webster was born in 1782 and served as a United States senator from Massachusetts and as a United States secretary of state.

ABOVE: John Brown, the fervent anti-slavery campaigner, was born in this house—photographed in 1900—in Torrington, Connecticut, in 1800. Brown gained notoriety for starting the violent Harper's Ferry rebellion against slavery in 1859.

and Sam Adams were from Boston. So was Benjamin Franklin. Crispus Attucks was from Framingham, and John Hancock and his flourishing autograph were from Braintree. John Quincy Adams grew up there, too. Even in colonial days, the men from Massachusetts had the reputation of being the most liberal in the colonies, a political label that has stuck. Ironically, much later the state that rebelled against excessive taxation without representation was sarcastically termed "Taxachusetts." For some, a modern response meant fleeing across the New Hampshire border to establish residency and commuting to jobs in Boston. New Hampshire had no state income tax.

Most of New England did not possess the same sort of left-wing reputation as Massachusetts. Maine, Vermont, and New Hampshire were picky about hippies in their communities and were outwardly austere in their lifestyles, as well as being regular churchgoers on Sunday. However, if there was a conservative streak running through many of the people of the region, there was also a deep-rooted sense of right and wrong. On May 18, 1652, well ahead of freedom from Great Britain, the leaders of Rhode

ABOVE: The home of John Quincy Adams, president of the United States from 1825 to 1829, who hailed from Massachusetts. His father, John Adams, preceded him in office from 1797 to 1801.

Island passed the first law in North America prohibiting slavery.

New Englanders have been accused of being too inwardly focused. A standing joke in Boston journalism was that if thousands of people were killed in a London bombing when a Bostonian was vacationing there, the *Boston Globe* headline would read, "Hub Man Fine In English Blast."

While literature produced by Louisa May Alcott, Robert Benchley, Emily Dickinson, e.e. cummings, Ralph Waldo Emerson, Dr. Seuss, and Anne Sexton might have redeeming social value, the Hub passed through a phase when it was best known for the unflattering phrase "Banned in Boston." And horror of horrors, in 1956, when Grace Metalious wrote a steamy novel, set in a

ABOVE: The energetic Teddy Roosevelt, president of the United States, on a visit to Concord, New Hampshire, in 1902, where he is making his feelings known about an issue of the day.

ABOVE RIGHT: The deaf and blind Helen Keller (seated) attended Radcliffe College in Cambridge, Massachusetts. She inspired generations with her devotion to living as normal a life as possible and was famously tutored by Anne Sullivan Macy.

composite New Hampshire town, the good fathers positively foamed at the mouth over the controversially explicit *Peyton Place*.

New England's most esteemed man of letters in the twentieth century was probably Robert Frost, who strung words together in poetry rather than popular fiction. Frost was eleven when his family moved from San Francisco to Lawrence,

ABOVE: Grace Metalious, seated at her typewriter, was a New Hampshire resident who created a sensation when she wrote the steamy best-seller *Peyton Place*, set in a fictitious small town in New Hampshire. In this 1956 photo, her husband George stands next to her.

ABOVE RIGHT: Lady Bird Johnson (on the left) was welcomed at the Kennedy compound in Cape Cod by Jacqueline Kennedy in August of 1960, while their husbands were seeking the nation's two highest offices.

Massachusetts, and he eventually resided in New Hampshire. There he became the most articulate of spokesmen for rural life, winning the Pulitzer Prize four times. For decades he wrote in Franconia, New Hampshire, and taught at Middlebury College in Vermont. He once said he could sum up everything he had learned about life in three words: "It goes on." After his death in 1963, Frost was depicted on a ten-cent stamp. He is buried in Vermont, a state that includes presidents Chester A. Arthur and Calvin Coolidge on its list of famous natives.

ABOVE: White-haired Robert Frost at a state dinner thrown by President John F. Kennedy in 1962. Frost, who lived in Massachusetts and divided his later writing and teaching years between New Hampshire and Vermont, won four Pulitzer Prizes for his poetry.

ABOVE: An idyllic setting in Boston about 1906, in front of the Massachusetts state capitol building.

ABOVE LEFT: Showing how early New Englanders lived from the land, this exhibit of a woman operating a spinning wheel is part of a Museum of Sciences and Industry display in Plymouth, Massachusetts.

LEFT: No Nintendo for these boys in Providence, Rhode Island, in 1912. They often amused themselves by pitching pennies on the sidewalks when they weren't attending school.

OPPOSITE: New Englanders can be conservative in their lifestyles. Beach attire was hardly risqué in 1900, with little exposed flesh besides faces, arms, and a few lower legs, but Rhode Islanders flocked to the shore anyway to beat the heat. This painting shows the beach at Narragansett Pier.

Poetry must run in the blood of northern New Englanders, since Henry Wadsworth Longfellow and Edna St. Vincent Millay were from Maine. The master of horror fiction, Stephen King, was born in Maine and in adulthood settled in Bangor. A string of others from the state has also achieved in the arts, though many left their small towns to do so. Director John Ford, actress Liv Tyler, and actor Judd Nelson gained fame in Hollywood. Perhaps the state's most famous athlete is long-distance runner Joan Benoit-Samuelson of Cape Elizabeth, who not only earned admiration for her grit and determination in overcoming injury, but won the Boston marathon in 1979 at her first attempt..

Connecticut has always done well by its inventors, visionaries, and financiers, from J. P. Morgan, who at one point

ABOVE: Worshippers file slowly into a church on Star Island, in New Hampshire, for a Sunday service in 1922.

ABOVE: With Bostonian Susan B. Anthony leading the charge, the women of New England fought hard for the right to vote. They campaigned from political offices such as this one in Newport, Rhode Island, seen in 1914.

LEFT AND ABOVE: For the rich and famous, New England was a restful playground. These high society ladies from New York are dressed up to enjoy the Twenties party lifestyle in Newport, Rhode Island.

ABOVE: Waterfront property, whether it is along Cape Cod in Massachusetts, the tougher Maine coast, or in Connecticut like this town, Stonington, seen in 1940, is very desirable to New Englanders.

LEFT: The Bleecher Street School was a symbol of America's melting pot in 1942. The student body, seen here observing Memorial Day, was half Polish-American and half Italian-American.

ABOVE: A Boy Scout troop whooping it up in New Bedford, Massachusetts, in 1942, perhaps earning a merit badge for singing.

ABOVE: The American flag is flying at half staff during a Memorial Day observance in Southington, Connecticut, in 1942. Marchers throng the main street for a parade.

TOP AND ABOVE: The federal government funded this eighty-unit housing project in 1942 for Bantam, Connecticut, workers devoting their efforts to a key World War II manufacturing facility nearby.

seemed to own the entire world, to Noah Webster, the author of the dictionary that bears his name, who seemed to know every word. For decades, Samuel Colt creatively improved shooters' aims with his pistols, and Frederick Law Olmsted improved the lands into parks.

Despite not being a terrifically large state, New Hampshire boasts an interesting roster of notable natives or important residents. These range from one-time president Franklin Pierce to reclusive author J. D. Salinger, from renowned documentary maker Ken Burns and astronaut Alan B. Shepard Jr. to painter Maxfield Parrish or Hall of Fame baseball catcher Carlton Fisk.

Ivy League Dartmouth College is one of the nation's elite universities, but was also the apparent inspiration for the school in the movie *Animal House*. John Knowles set his bittersweet classic novel, *A Separate Peace*, at a Phillips Exeter Academy–like place.

Rhode Island has had its moments with show business, producing hoofer and songster George M. Cohan, funny man Buddy Hackett, and the singing group the Cowsills, not a trio of acts expected to appear on the same stage at the same time.

LEFT: A thriving community, Provincetown, on the tip of Cape Cod, is known for its beaches. In this 1942 photograph, members of a church's congregation are walking home after a service.

If they ever had, one could only wish that portrait painter Gilbert Stuart could have been alive for the moment to depict the scene.

It is, however, Boston and its surrounding area that has produced more historically significant individuals than any other locale in New England. Samuel Morse of Charlestown, for example, invented the telegraph, Eli Whitney of Westborough created the cotton gin, and Salem resident Alexander Graham Bell invented the telephone. Henry David Thoreau of Concord urged people to think about preserving nature before industrialization could wipe it out. Jack Kerouac of Lowell stuck his thumb out, hitchhiking around America, and jump-started another revolution, this one among restless young people who wanted to see their country up close after reading his book *On the Road*.

Leonard Bernstein of Cambridge gave the world great music. Jack Lemmon and Leonard Nimoy of Boston, and Lee Remick of Quincy, produced memorable images on flickering screens. So did Harvard graduate Erich Segal's book and flick *Love Story*, which made so many weep. An attorney named George V. Higgins made a dramatic career change when he penned *The Friends of Eddie Coyle* in 1972 and became popular for his realistic, hard-nosed dialogue in Bostonian voices.

Sports heroes often took center stage. Red Sox leftfielder Ted Williams, perhaps the best hitter who ever lived, dominated the baseball landscape from 1939 until his retirement in 1960. Bob Cousy was beloved at Holy Cross in the early 1950s, even before he joined the Celtics.

Always there was heroism or big ideas. Clara Barton of Oxford brought mercy to the battlefield, and Susan B. Anthony of Adams sought to make the world fair for women. Bringing justice for all was a role that the Kennedy family of Cambridge and Hyannis embraced. If Massachusetts—and the rest of New England—was seduced by

ABOVE: A man and his young helpers drag a net toward the shore in Narragansett Bay, Rhode Island, hoping to stock up on bait so they can go after bigger fish.

OPPOSITE, TOP: A group of female students enjoys the comfortable weather on the steps of the Waterman Building at the University of Vermont in Burlington, in about 1950. All are wearing skirts—despite the New England commitment to women's rights, it was too soon for slacks to be socially acceptable.

OPPOSITE, BOTTOM: Neighborliness is at the heart of the New England character. A group of neighbors in Wilbraham, Massachusetts, in 1955 demonstrate this by rebuilding a house for the Harvey family after their home was lost to fire.

royalty as a role model nearly two centuries after independence from the king of England, it was the fault of the extended Kennedy clan. John F. Kennedy, and his dazzling wife Jacqueline Bouvier, ascended to the White House in 1960. Robert F. Kennedy, later senator from New York (because a brother already had one of two seats from Massachusetts), became a symbol of hope for the downtrodden. And beginning in 1962, Ted Kennedy matured into one of the most important senators in

ABOVE: The clerks at the Vallee Drugstore in Westbrook, Maine, where 1930s crooner Rudy Vallee grew up, gathered unexpected attention on the periphery of a gossipy marriage dispute between Vallee and his wife.

RIGHT: In the late 1960s, America obsessed over the hair length of its teenage sons and rigid sides were taken. This Norwalk, Connecticut, billboard was an offshoot of a 1968 legal case. Four boys were suspended from school for wearing long hair and they challenged the matter in court.

U.S. history. The Kennedys gave lives to public service, and Massachusetts and New England have always been beholden, respectful, and appreciative.

The Kennedys, like the Red Sox and the heroes of the Revolutionary War, helped unify New England. Though the rugged mountains of New Hampshire and Vermont and the rugged coastline of Maine seem to have little in common with the heavily trafficked interstates of Massachusetts, Connecticut, and Rhode Island, a shared heritage, a shared history, and a shared pride in the region have trumped all of the differences. As did a Red Sox World Series title in 2004, ending eighty-six years of misery and paying a rich dividend for all those New Englanders who had suffered repeated defeats from the 1920s through the 1970s and beyond.

ABOVE: Perhaps the greatest unifier of the New England states is the passionate support for the Boston Red Sox baseball team—for so long afflicted by the "curse of the Bambino" that saw the team miss out on a World Championship pennant for decades after the sale of Babe Ruth (left) to the Yankees in 1919.

SPORTS AND LEISURE

From the infant days of the twentieth century, baseball was America's national pastime. The Boston Red Sox came along in 1901. Later the team was savvy enough to broadcast its games throughout the region, and game tickets were always available if you drove into Boston from Vermont, New Hampshire, Connecticut, Maine, or Rhode Island, so the Red Sox became universal regional property. Since there were no other major professional teams in the five other New England states, Massachusetts had to share.

The Sox arrived on automobile radios and on living room TV sets with the first scent of spring and lingered until after school began. The great Curt Gowdy, on his way to an esteemed broadcasting career, was the play-by-play voice. It was like listening to your buddy fill you in on the hits, runs, and errors. When Curt paused on baseball, he tried to sell you a beer. "Hello neighbor, have a 'Gansett," is the way the Narragansett, Rhode Island, company's ads went, making listeners

ABOVE: The dome of the Connecticut state capitol building in Hartford gleams in the sunlight and looms above Bushnell Park, the nation's oldest park created with public funds.

"New England's parlor, a region's nightclub, and the Olde Towne Team's hearth."

Curt Smith in *Our House: A Tribute to Fenway Park* (1999).

LEFT: Riding the rides, playing the midway games, eating the delicious, fattening food, and just gazing at the people as you walk around are all fun-filled aspects of touring the Vermont State Fair in Rutland.

ABOVE: The crowds swarm the grounds at the Blue Hill Fair in Blue Hill, Maine, sometime between 1890 and 1920.

ABOVE: A bit formal for a canoeing trip, but that was the nature of modest dress in the 1880s and 1890s in mixed company. There were no exceptions, even for a paddle on Moosehead Lake in Maine.

BELOW: Come on in, the water's fine. A group of youngsters swim, splash, and cool themselves down in a stream during the summer in Connecticut.

LEFT: On hot summer days, New Englanders have always fled to their beaches to bask in the sea breezes, as in this scene at York Beach in Maine in 1901.

ABOVE: Even with the ocean a few steps away, young people were fascinated and thrilled by water slides when they began springing up at resort areas in the twentieth century. Zipping down the slide, like this one at Old Orchard Beach in Maine, provided a rush that was hard to duplicate.

think of the Red Sox and Narragansett in the same sentence.

The remarkable aspect of New England's proprietary grasp of the Red Sox, and of the Red Sox hold on New Englanders, was that the team was not very good most of the time. The Red Sox accounted for a World Series triumph in 1918 but two years later made the mistake of the century, trading Babe Ruth to the New York Yankees. Many New Englanders despised New York. Yes, Connecticut abutted New York, but for northern New Englanders in particular, ancient maps might as well have read, "Beyond there be dragons." The purest common ground between New Englanders of Maine, Vermont, and New Hampshire with those of Massachusetts, Rhode Island, and Connecticut, besides snowstorms, was shared agony over the fate of the Red Sox. As the years, then decades passed, young people growing up in New England reminded each other of the last championship and said, "The Red Sox will win in my lifetime." Many were wrong. Red Sox losing had staying power and so did fan angst.

As the Red Sox slumped, Fenway Park

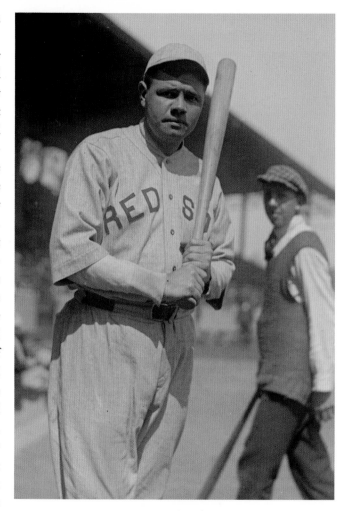

ABOVE: Babe Ruth, the most revered slugger of all time, made his mark as a pitcher with the Boston Red Sox before gaining greater fame with the New York Yankees, after a trade that disillusioned Hub fans.

ABOVE: These twenty-three African-American men made up a Danbury, Connecticut, area baseball team in 1880, a time when a handful of black players made their way into the majors before being banned later.

RIGHT: Workmen hurry to complete construction of the bleachers section of Fenway Park in Boston in 1912. The Red Sox won the World Series that year.

endured. Built in 1912, the baseball palace aged, was considered an outdated relic, and then enjoyed a renaissance as a magnificent exemplar of times gone by. Kenmore Square's signature Citgo sign, originally erected in 1940 to advertise the Texas-based gasoline company, was almost as closely identified with the ballpark as the Green Monster fence in left field. Opened the same week the *Titanic* sank (many felt that was no coincidence), Fenway Park became the oldest stadium in the major leagues and to the faithful it was a holy secular shrine unmatched anywhere in the six states. Once upon a time a ticket cost a dollar and viewing games from center field represented a rite of passage for New England youngsters.

Fans were not as passionate about the Boston Celtics pro basketball team despite its success with Bill Russell, Bill Sharman, Tommy Heinsohn, and Bob Cousy, or the Boston Bruins hockey team, But those winter sports clubs did belong to New England, too. In 1971, when they shifted headquarters from Boston to Foxboro, Massachusetts (close to the Rhode Island state line), the Boston Patriots energized their regional fan base by changing the team name to New

OPPOSITE, TOP: Fenway Park, home of the Boston Red Sox baseball team, opened in 1912 and this is the structure that greeted fans in 1914. The Red Sox are the hometown team of all of New England.

OPPOSITE, BOTTOM: Fans flock to Braves Field for the ground's opening-day game against the St. Louis Cardinals on August 18, 1915. Specially chartered trains were used to transport fans to the event, though many chose to drive in their new automobiles.

ABOVE: Fenway Park is now one of the most famous landmarks in New England. The Citgo sign looming over the "Green Monster" left-field wall is almost as famous. The sign for the gasoline company has been standing in Kenmore Square since 1940.

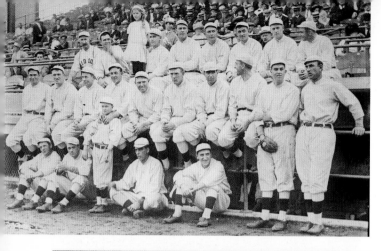

BOSTON NATIONAL BLOOMER GIRL'S BASE BALL CLUB.   L. J. GALBREATH, Originator and Owner.

TOP: The Boston Red Sox were a baseball powerhouse in the first part of the twentieth century, playing in fabled Fenway Park and capturing the hearts of New Englanders. Here, the famous 1912 World Series winners who defeated the Yankees 3–2 in one of the closest contests ever.

ABOVE: You didn't have to be a guy to play ball. The Boston Bloomer Girls baseball team represented the area in women's competition. Here, team owner L. J. Galbreath poses with his charges.

England Patriots. Boston also had the annual Beanpot hockey tournament, which put Boston University, Boston College, Harvard, and Northeastern at one another's throats.

Around the region, strong allegiances formed with local universities, from Vermont's hockey and basketball teams, to Maine's baseball team and, above all, the University of Connecticut's men's and women's basketball teams. The Huskie women's superiority and fame spread and made women's basketball trendy long before it caught on elsewhere.

New Englanders have always been at peace with snowfall, and weekend getaways took downhill skiers to Waterville Valley or Crotched Mountain in New Hampshire or Sugarloaf in Maine. Devotees of winter sports have also flocked to the Laconia World Championship Sled Dog Races in New Hampshire for multi-day sprint races since 1929.

For those who enjoyed another form of competitive racing, Laconia also hosted Motorcycle Week in June each year. More people rode than mushed—attendance eventually reached into the six figures. In 1916, a few hundred motorcycle riders gathered at Weir Beach, and in 1923 the

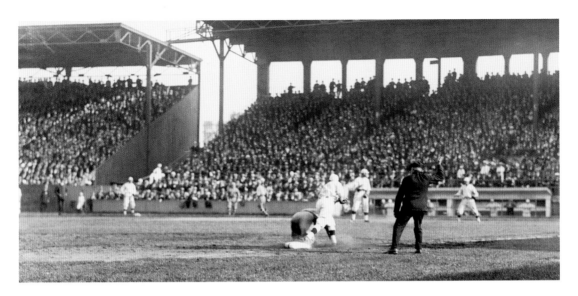

Federation of American Motorcyclists first gave them their stamp of approval. There was a bump in the road in 1965 when motorcycle gangs and police battled, but the original fun spirit of the event was soon recaptured.

Rhode Island really was the Ocean State when hosting the America's Cup international challenge races between 1930 and 1983 in Newport. Residents who loved to catch the wind in their faces, throw up their sails, and head for the sea, for a half century bore witness to the best 12-meter sailboat racing in the world. Yachts with the names *Intrepid, Courageous,* and *Freedom*

ABOVE: The Red Sox won their last World Series for eighty-six years in 1918 by defeating the Chicago Cubs. It was later suggested that the Sox were forever paying for the foolish error of trading Babe Ruth and so suffered from the "Curse of the Bambino."

still live on in local lore and Rhode Islanders well remember when the state was overrun by thousands and thousands of spectators for the events.

Puritanical in thought from the start, New England was not usually in the forefront of groundbreaking dance steps. Jazz and swing did infiltrate, however, from the 1930s on, and such clubs as Wally's Paradise, Paul's Mall, The Hi Hat, and the Savoy Ballroom were gathering places for cutting-edge risk takers who liked to kick up their heels.

One highbrow pastime that can challenge the Red Sox as a local institution is

ABOVE: These fancily dressed spectators were on hand in New London, Connecticut, for a Harvard-Yale crew competition in 1920. Harvard captured the contest.

ABOVE: A mother and daughter promenade on the grounds of the tennis club at Newport, Rhode Island, in 1922 where an invitational tournament was taking place. Newport later became home to the International Tennis Hall of Fame.

classical music. The Boston Symphony Orchestra, founded in 1885, is the most prestigious formal musical organization of the region, playing regular concerts at Symphony Hall. In summer, a segment of the orchestra, known as the Boston Pops (first directed by Arthur Fiedler in 1930 and for a half century after), plays free outdoor concerts at the Charles River Esplanade.

When television was in its infancy, on weekdays Big Brother Bob Emery hosted a TV program for youngsters and at noontime used a glass of milk to toast a portrait of President Dwight Eisenhower. Rex Trailer and his horse Goldrush on *Boomtown* made Saturdays special. He was an honest-to-goodness cowboy (what could be better?). Rex also sang and had a "Saddlebag O' Songs."

A big night out with the kids involved pulling into a double feature at the Mansfield Drive-In Theater in

ABOVE: In the early part of the twentieth century, some of the biggest powers in college football were Ivy League schools like Yale, here at practice in New Haven, Connecticut.

OPPOSITE: T.O.M. Sopwith's *Endeavor II*, skips across the waves, her white wings spread to the wind, as she trails Vanderbilt's *Ranger* to lose the best-of-seven America's Cup races at Newport, Rhode Island, in 1937. Newport was home to the races for a half century.

RIGHT: A poster announcing upcoming live entertainment in Salem, Massachusetts, heralds the appearance of ten vaudeville acts in 1938. Showing at the Now and Then Hall, the presentation was under the auspices of the Depression-era Federal Theatre Project.

RIGHT: They knew how to have fun at Dartmouth College. Rather than hide from winter's snow and ice, the Ivy League college celebrated the season with Winter Carnivals like this one in 1947.

FAR RIGHT: Fun in the sun—and a bit daring, too. Riding on the Ferris wheel at the Vermont State Fair in Rutland in 1941 could provide a stunning view when the wheel stopped and left you on top.

ABOVE: Fishing is popular throughout the New England states. Lakes and ponds are plentiful, and boys like these in Maine dropped many a line to bring home the local catch for dinner.

BELOW: Drive-in movie theaters proliferated throughout New England in the 1950s: some are still going strong. The sites also sometimes served a double purpose. On Sunday mornings such as this in 1951 in Dorchester, Massachusetts, church services were also held at the drive-ins.

Connecticut, or the Rustic Tri-View Drive-In Theater in North Smithfield, Rhode Island, where you could hang the squawk box on the car window for sound. Parents felt lucky if the kids, who came attired in their pajamas, fell asleep before the second picture.

The youthful memories of generations of Connecticut's kids would have been incomplete without a ride on the 1914 carousel at Bushnell Park in Hartford or a visit to 332-acre Lake Compounce in Bristol, the nation's oldest amusement park, founded in 1846. Yes, dad and grandma got to play there, too. Picnics, swimming, rowing, concerts, and roller coasters (the Wildcat has rolled since 1927) have long been staples.

Funtown/Splashtown's roots date back to 1959. The Saco, Maine, fun emporium features everything from bumper cars to the only wooden roller coaster in the state. The water park also has eighteen slides, the longest and tallest log flume ride in New England, an antique car display, and theme rides.

Not everyone in Vermont felt like making a couple-hour drive to Boston to watch the highly paid professionals ply their sports trades. Sports franchises for

LEFT: One of the most pleasant outdoor winter pursuits throughout New England is ice skating. The best skating is on frozen ponds or lakes, as these skaters in Brockton, Massachusetts, know.

minor leagues proliferated, and all seemed supremely aware of the Green Mountain State's local traditions and reputation. The baseball team in Burlington was dubbed the Vermont Lake Monsters (a nod to Lake Champlain) and the basketball team was called the Vermont Frost Heaves. The semi-pro football team was called the Vermont Ice Storm. Apparently there is no escaping the cold-weather image in Vermont.

Other parts of New England are more seasonably adapted. In Maine, an escape to Acadia National Park's 30,000-plus island acres has always been on the agenda. And in Massachusetts, the major league summer getaway is to Cape Cod, the eastern peninsula of the state. The Cape Cod League has been one of the premier summer baseball leagues for college players since the 1960s, though the most popular sport traditionally is guessing which players will make the majors some day.

Half of the challenge of getting to "The Cape" was braving Friday night traffic on Route 3. Even when the mileage was gentle, the traffic time was potentially brutal. But once in Barnstable, Provincetown, Sandwich, or Hyannis Port, the sand beneath the toes was always soothing.

LEFT: New Englanders had to put up with traffic jams, but it was worth it to escape from the city heat to the beaches each summer, as these Cape Cod sun worshippers found out in the 1960s.

ABOVE: The Boston Pops concerts on the Esplanade adjacent to the Charles River are very popular. The special New Year's Eve concert has been known to attract up to a million people.

BELOW: Boston Symphony Orchestra conductor Arthur Fiedler during a rehearsal at age eighty-four in 1979, just days before his fiftieth anniversary performance as the orchestra's leader.